Let's Sleep

Written by Jo Windsor

This monkey sleeps
in a tree.

This leopard sleeps
in a tree, too.

This bear sleeps
in a cave.

This bat sleeps
in a cave, too.

Badgers sleep
under the ground.

Rabbits sleep
under the ground, too.

This sea otter sleeps on the water.

This polar bear sleeps on the snow.

Mice sleep
in nests.

This orangutan sleeps
in a nest.

**Birds sleep
in nests, too.**

But these birds . . .

. . . sleep on one leg.

Index

▬▬ Guide Notes

Title: Let's Sleep
Stage: Early (1) – Red

Genre: Nonfiction (Expository)
Approach: Guided Reading
Processes: Thinking Critically, Exploring Language, Processing Information
Visual Focus: Photographs (static images)

THINKING CRITICALLY
(sample questions)
- What do you think this book is going to tell us?
- What do you know about how animals sleep?
- Focus the children's attention on the Index. Ask: "What animals are you going to find out about in this book?"
- If you want to find out about a leopard, what page would you look on?
- If you want to find out about a bear, what page would you look on?
- Look at pages 4 and 5. What are these animals doing that is the same?
- Which sleeping place do you think is the most interesting? Why?
- Which place could you sleep in?
- Which place would be the most difficult for you to sleep in? Why?

EXPLORING LANGUAGE

Terminology
Title, cover, photographs, author, photographers

Vocabulary
Interest words: badger, sea otter, orangutan
High-frequency words: this, in, a, too, the, on, but
Positional words: in, on, under

Print Conventions
Capital letter for sentence beginnings, periods, commas, ellipses